© 2009 by Edward Pappert and its licensors. All rights reserved.

No part of this book may be reproduced, stored in a retrieval system, or transmitted by any means, electronic, mechanical, photocopying, recording, or otherwise, without written permission from the author.

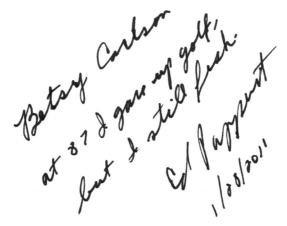

This book will help you:

Select the fishing gear.

Spin Casting Reel

Spinning Reel

A 6 foot Rod

How to tie the hook to the line.

Palomar Knot

Clinch Knot

What lures to use.

Texas Rig

Grass hopper

How to fish for:

Pumpkin Seed

Catfish

Large Mouth Bass

Yellow Perch

Walleye

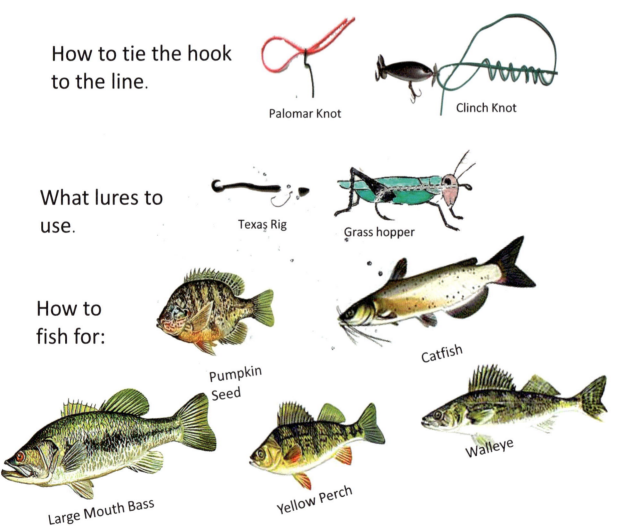

"Fish images copyrighted by www.identicards.com"

Many fishermen catch and release fish.

Rainbow Trout

Some have the fish mounted.

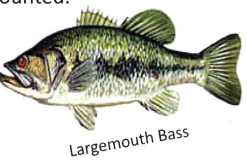

Largemouth Bass

Some fish are caught because they are good eating.

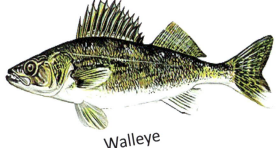

Walleye

The following slides will help you learn to catch a fish a sport you can enjoy for the rest of your life.

"Fish images copyrighted by www.identiCards.com"

Still Fishing

Start with "still fishing". You can use any type of rod (including a cane pole). Any weight line (suggest no. 6) a small hook, a weight and a bobber.

For bait a small worm, cricket, a piece of smelly cheese or any small insect.

The weight takes the bait down. The bobber keeps it from going to the bottom.

When the fish takes the bait, the bobber goes under and you jerk the line upward. This sets the hook. Just pull the fish in.

While any fish might strike, still fishing is used mostly to catch Sun Fish. They are fun to catch and are good eating.

If this is for a youngster, or if you have never fished and want the easiest fishing gear, then buy a kit.

Shakespeare ©, Zebco ©, and others have inexpensive kits that are of good quality .

      These kits have everything needed to catch fish.

Sean caught this flounder with a minnow

Eddie caught this on a minnow.

Bob caught this Bass on a plastic worm.

Bobbers are used when still fishing.

They serve two basic functions.

1. They keep the bait off the bottom.
2. When they go under the water you know a fish has taken the bait.

Select the right bobber for the kind of fishing you plan to do. The bobber must float just enough so that it is not pulled under by the weight.

If the bobber is too big, the fish will feel resistance. When the fish tugs at the bait and it seems to tug back because of too much resistance from the bobber the fish may leave.

When in doubt use the smaller bobber.

Spin casting reel

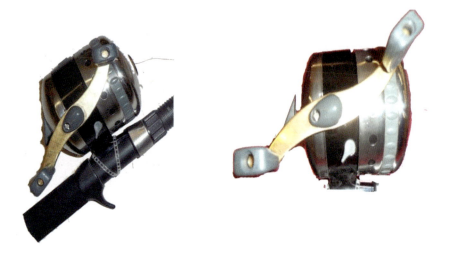

Recommended for youngsters

Holding the rod at the base with your thumb on a "thumb-button," a cast is made. It is just like throwing a ball . The "thumb-button" is released just as the ball would leave your fingers.

The best feature of this reel is-It will never backlash.

Spinning Reel

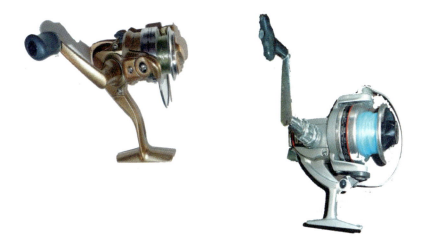

A very popular reel as it is easy to use (with a little practice). Long casts can be made with light lures.

Casting with a rod and reel

With a little practice, casting permits you to place your bait much further away than still fishing.

When practicing casting, choose an open space with no overhanging bushes or trees. Put on an object the size and weight of a lure but without hooks.

After casting, let the lure sink, then reel it in slowly.

Spin Casting Reel

Highly recommended for beginners and youngsters. Holding the rod at the base with your thumb on the "thumb button," a cast is made similar to throwing a ball. Release the thumb button just as you would release the ball.

The best feature of this reel is that it will never backlash.

Spinning Reel

Most experienced fishermen prefer the spinning reel. It can cast further than the spinning casting reel with a much lighter lure.

It also has a "drag". This permits the setting of resistance the line has when the fish is fighting.

Choosing a rod.

Don't be confused by the great number and types of fishing rods that are available.

For fishing lakes, ponds, and rivers, get a flexible reel that is 6 to 7 feet in length.

There are many reasonably priced rods that are of good quality.

The sales person in the fishing department is usually very knowledgeable and will help you.

Hooks and Lures

Hooks come in all sizes and many shapes.

Lures also come in many sizes and shapes. Many of the lures seem to be better at catching fishermen than fish.

The type of hook and/or lure suggested to catch fish will be discussed as each type of fish is shown.

A spin casting reel

Always comes with fishing line.

A spinning reel

Usually comes with fishing line, If not, put the line on. A number 6 test line is a good one to use.
Talk to the salesperson. He or she can advise you. They will either put the line on for you or at least tell you how.

There are small hooks

Treble hooks

Special hooks for bass

Hooks used with artificial lures

Tying the hook or lure to the line.

While there are many knots.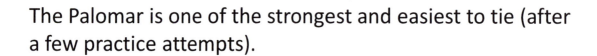

The Palomar is one of the strongest and easiest to tie (after a few practice attempts).

The Palomar Knot is used when the line is tied directly to the hook.

When attaching a lure to the line, the Clinch Knot is recommended.

The following picture shows how each of these knots are tied.

Clinch Knot

Step 1

Thread the line through the hook or the lure.

Step 2

Twist the free end 6 or 7 times around the line.

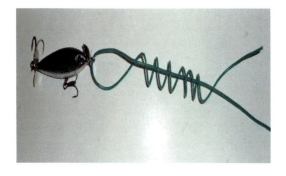

Step 3

Pass the free end between the eye of the hook and the first loop.

Step 4

Pull out all of the slack, then pull tightly. Trim the loose end.

The Palomar Knot

Step 1.
Double about 6 inches of line and pass it through the eye of the hook.

Step 2
Tie an overhand knot in the double line. The hook should be at the bottom

The Palomar Knot is one of the easiest to tie and is one of the strongest

Step 3

Bring t the he hook through line.

Step 4

Pull the line tight and clip off any extra line.

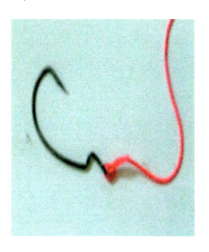

I thought fish liked minnows, crickets, worms and grasshoppers.

And this is the way you put them on the hook.

But I don't want to touch a worm.

You don't have to. Dad says a plastic worm works just as well. And it's not icky.

Many fisherman use the "Texas Rig" when fishing for Bass.

Thread the line through a "Bullet" shaped weight. Then tie on the hook using the Palomar knot.

Push the hook into the head of the plastic worm then bring it out about a half inch back from the head.

Rotate the hook and push the point into the body of the worm.

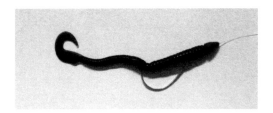

When rigged the worm should be straight.
(Purple worms seem to be best.)

Bluegill, Brim, Bream, Sunfish

All are similar, named as they fit into a frying pan.

Pumpkin Seed

Redbreast Sunfish

Yellow Perch

They are pan fish.

- To fish for this type of fish, use a small hook.
- Worms, grasshoppers, crickets, minnows, beetles or an artificial lure work best.
- Put a weight about 10 inches from the hook.
- Use a bobber
- Fish close to shore

"Fish images copyrighted by www.identiCards.com"

Largemouth Bass

There is a special hook.

And a special weight.

The weight is shaped like a bullet. The weight keeps the lure on the bottom. The shape of the weight helps keep the lure from catching in the weeds.

"Fish images copyrighted by www.identiCards.com"

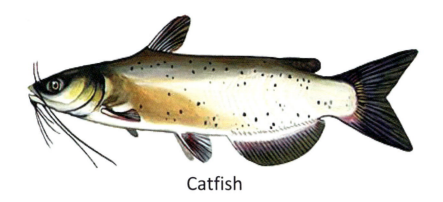

Catfish

Catfish are in some lakes, but mostly in slow moving waters.

They bite early in the morning, in the evening, or at night.

They bite on natural types of bait such a earthworms, chunks of meat, chunks of fish or minnows.

Catfish in lakes can be small. In slow moving waters they can weigh up to 150 pounds.

Like most fish their size, they are in direct proportion to the size of body in which they live.

The important thing is to put the bait on the bottom. Catfish have a good sense of smell.

Smelly cheese or garlicky pieces of hot dogs make good bait.

"Fish images copyrighted by www.identiCards.com"

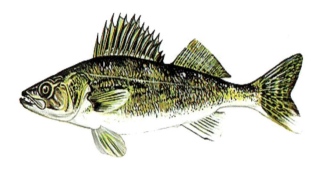

Walleye

Many fishermen fish for Walleyes, only as they are very good eating.

Walleyes are a school fish, so when one is caught, there will be others in the area.

No special tackle is needed. A light weight rod will make fishing fun.

Slow trolling is a good way to find schools of Walleye. Use a no. 6 Hook.

Minnows, night crawlers, and leeches are the preferred bait. The best thing to do is ask at the bait shop as to what they are biting on at the time.

Most of the time Walleyes are in deep water requiring a weight.

Unlike Bass, Walleyes have a soft bite, if you think you feel a tug set the hook.

"Fish images copyrighted by www.identicards.com"

If you want to catch a big fish, then you should fish for a Carp.

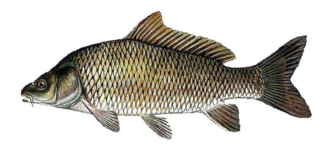

The fish you see jumping out of the water and making a large splash are probably Carp.

Carp are finicky eaters, therefore hard to catch.
They are bottom feeders.
Use a no. 6 hook and a single kernel of corn, a green pea or a smelly piece of cheese.

Put the hook onto a monofilament leader at least a yard long.

They put up a good fight, therefore fun to catch.

After you catch one, I recommend you cut it up and use it for fertilizer for your garden . Although eaten in Europe the Carp is not considered good eating.

I would not return the Carp to the lake as Carp root on the bottom and destroy the habitat of the other fish.

Picture by: Duane Raver/US Fish and Wildlife Service   credit Duane Raver/usfws

Hi, I'm Lindsey.
My sister Lauren, the twins Gannon and Agee think I'm too little to fish.

I can fish. I just need someone to bait the hook, put on the bobber and cast it out into the lake.

When the bobber goes under the water, I will jerk the fishing rod and pull in the fish.

Everyone wants to catch a big fish. Not me. I want to catch a real small one, put it into a fish bowl and have a pet fish.

"Fish images copyrighted by www.identiCards.com"

Things to take with you when you go fishing.

A small knife with scissors to trim the line.

Forceps or small needle-nosed pliers to remove the hook .

A stringer to hold the fish is needed if you plan to keep the fish.

Things needed are handy

A carpenters apron that holds the above plus a few extra hooks and lures.

No need to carry a tackle box

Many people wish you good luck when you go fishing.

Luck has very little to do with your ability to catch fish.

Like everything else, observe what works well.

Ask good fisherman what they do.

The internet and the library have a lot of information that will make you a good fisherman.

"Fish images copyrighted by identicards.com"

But for now just go fishing and enjoy!

Made in the USA
Charleston, SC
09 August 2010